RECEIVING PERSONAL PROPHECY

RECEIVING PERSONAL PROPHECY

Prophetic Keys to Unlocking Your Prophecies

BILL VINCENT

Revival Waves of Glory

Receiving Personal Prophecy
Copyright © 2016 by Bill Vincent. All rights reserved.

No part of this publication may be reproduced, stored in a retrieval system or transmitted in any way by any means, electronic, mechanical, photocopy, recording or otherwise without the prior permission of the author except as provided by USA copyright law.

Published in the United States of America
ISBN: 978-1-62676-927-4
1. Religion / Christian Life / Spiritual Growth
2. Religion / Christian Life / Personal Growth
14.07.15

TABLE OF CONTENTS

BOOK DISCLAIMER 7

INTRODUCTION 9
WAR FOR YOUR WORDS 11
GOD IS SPEAKING 13
HOLY PROPHECY 24
WHY WE NEED PROPHETIC MINISTRY 25
THE HEART OF THE PROPHETIC PERSON 27
REJECTION AND PRIDE ISSUES 29
TRUE AND COUNTERFEIT PROPHETS 31
COMMON STUMBLING BLOCKS 32
GOD SPEAKS TO US THROUGH HIS WORD 36
DOING WHAT WE HEAR GOD SAY 38
DEFINING PROPHECY 41
RESPONDING TO PROPHECY 44
PROPHETIC LANGUAGE 49
GIFTS AND CALLING 53
OUR RESPONSE 56
PROPHETIC PERSONALITY 60
PROPHETIC MOUTHPIECE 63
RELATIONSHIPS 70
GOD'S WAY 72
CAREFUL DECISIONS 80
UNDERSTANDING PROPHETIC 81
KEEP RECORD 83
REMOVING HINDRANCES 87
FINAL WORD 93

ABOUT THE AUTHOR 97

RECOMMENDED BOOKS 99

BOOK DISCLAIMER

Here are tips on reading Bill Vincent's Books.

Bill writes prophetically as God speaks. The grammar may be pushed but the message is spoken from the heart of God. Bill didn't want to lose the depth of revelation through extensive editing.

INTRODUCTION

Over twenty years I have been in the prophetic ministry. There have been a lot of lessons I've learned from years of ministry and surrounding myself with prophetic people. This book is Volume Two of my prophetic book series. You can get Volume One "Increasing Your Prophetic Gift" if you would like to learn to flow in a deeper level of prophetic.

This book is for everyone who has been around the prophetic and has ever received a prophetic Word. I'm talking about mostly personal prophetic ministry, where some one singles you out and prophesies to you personally. This also will be a great tool for receiving a Word for a Church, City, Country or so on. This book has the basic guidelines and the strategies for bringing your Words to pass.

Over the years I have received hundreds of prophecies and up through 2010 they have all come to pass. I mean that ALL my personal prophecies have been fulfilled. This is by using the guidelines and strategies I'm writing in this book. So fasten your seat belt as you read "Receiving Personal Prophecy."

WAR FOR YOUR WORDS

The enemy hears the Word also, so usually things go the opposite way of what God Says.

People should not hold personal conversations with a Prophet, or anything you want to hear from God. You should never tell a Prophet. A true prophetic Word should come from God and it should be prophetic not pathetic if a true Prophet hears from God and has a Word for you then he will not have to ask you any questions.

God qualifies the ones that He calls. He does not call the qualified. He calls those that have been through the trenches. If you haven't been through anything then how could you minister to those that are going through the trenches? God also does not use quitters. You have to be prepared to finish the race because if you are not you will go around the mountain until you do not quit or give up.

A prophetic Word speaks potential it is not a guarantee, this is why we war for our Words and not only warring but contending for God to move on our behalf and we also have to line up to the Word that He speaks we can't expect God to do great things on our behalf when we are living like the devil.

If you are not going to do anything with the first Word God gave you don't ask for another one, although God is full of grace and mercy and He will probably give you another one. God is good and He is faithful. There will come a time when He will want you to do something to get another Word from the Lord you will sooner or later have to line up and do something with the ones he has already given you.

Some prophetic Words are seasonal which means if you don't go after them when they are in season, then sometimes we miss them and God will usually bring them around our path again in another season but you will probably need to repent for not doing your part maybe you missed it because you didn't hear correctly or maybe you didn't line up or maybe it was because someone else didn't line up who really knows when we all get to Heaven we will know what we missed and why. We will probably all find out how much more we could have had here on Earth if maybe we might of done something a little different. We all have fallen short of something.

Everything you will ever do for God comes with a hefty price to pay and you will pay it or you will not do much for Him.

This is one reason I'm writing this book. This book is to help you see the finished work of your prophetic Words.

GOD IS SPEAKING

God desires to have intimate fellowship with individuals. God speaks every minute of every day but His people are dull of hearing.

God wants to speak to us through prophecy but we must read His Word. Many Christians go after prophetic words.

The apostle Paul writes in 1 Timothy 4:14-15, "Do not neglect the gift that is in you, which was given to you through prophecy with the laying on of hands by the council of elders. Put these things into practice, devote yourself to them, so that all may see your progress."

Personal prophecy, as Paul mentions here, is for the upbuilding and encouragement of individual Christians, and of the Church at large. It was true in the First Century, and it is still true in the day we live in.

But like none of the other spiritual gifts mentioned in the New Testament, personal prophecy has the greatest ability to bring edification on the one hand and to damage on the other hand—based on how the believer responds to the prophetic word.

To help people properly engage with New Testament prophecy, I have listed some practical ways that a believer in the modern-day church can and should respond to a personal prophetic word. Record, Read and Meditate upon the Word

It is recommended that all prophetic words be recorded and that they should be transcribed and kept for future reference. These words can then be reviewed with one's pastor or spiritual covering as a means of counseling and as a way to track spiritual growth.

When reviewing a prophecy, it should be noted that not every element of the word will be applicable to the recipient's present experience. In 1 Thessalonians 5:19-21, the apostle Paul writes, "Do not quench the Spirit. Do not despise the words of prophets, but test everything; hold fast to what is good." This Scripture warns us to prove and judge prophecy, not the prophet, if some elements may not seem to relate at the present time. If a person does not understand a portion of a prophetic utterance they should be careful not to reject it immediately as false. It may be that the word refers to something that is yet to come in the person's life and they do not yet have knowledge of it. Instead, the person should put the word "on the shelf" for prayerful consideration at a later time.

Witness To and then War a Good Warfare with the Word In the proving process, we accept and receive that which is timely and deals with the past or present in an accurate way. 1 Timothy 1:18 tells us to prepare for warfare with God's prophetic words to us at hand; "I am giving you these instructions, Timothy, my child, in accordance with the prophecies made earlier about you, so that by following them you may fight the good fight..."

Do Nothing Different unless Definitely Directed By God When a prophetic word refers to transitions in life such as romance, geographical moves, changing churches, and so forth, it is important that a person never make hasty changes until prayer, godly counsel and much reflections are made. Through careful prayer, counsel with spiritual leadership and cautious small steps of faith, God's purposes can be established in the believer's life.

The Bible gives many examples of caution in the face of a prophetic word. We see in 1 Samuel 16:13 that David tended sheep for many years after being told he would be king. Jehu received very specific instructions in his anointing as king concerning what he was to do in 2 Kings 9. King Jehoshaphat was shown in 2 Chronicles 20 to follow all the divine directives in detail. It is imperative that we not only hear God's word, but also listen for the way and the timing on how that word is to be fulfilled.

Remove All Hindrances to Receiving the Promise When dealing with personal prophecy, a Christian must be willing to judge him or herself to make certain they are able to hear from God. Attitudes that can hinder our hearing from the Lord include negative mind-sets, an inflated or a low self-image, pride, self-justification, blame-shifting, self-preservation, people-pleasing, carnal reasoning and procrastination. Hidden or unconfessed sin or unforgiveness can also hinder our ability to hear from God.

A biblical example of a person needing to judge himself was King Saul. When the promises of God were presented to him, he rationalized God's directives and chose what he wanted. This brought about God's judgment on his life and he never received the promises of God (1 Samuel 15).

Wait Patiently upon the Lord We are told in Isaiah 40:31 to wait patiently upon the Lord. The principle of waiting on the Lord is found throughout Scripture. The biblical meaning of waiting is active, expectant faith.

Allow God to Form Character in the Process God's primary intent in the life of the believer is to call leaders and to test every area of their lives in preparation for ministry. Prophecies given to us about future ministry should be received with joy, and with respect for the process God will use to prepare us for that leadership.

Men in the Bible like David, Joseph, Abraham and Moses were tested first before they were given dynamic ministries. Women like Deborah, Esther and Priscilla showed themselves to be women of character. God developed these people through testing, trying and time.

The foundation of a person's character will determine the height of the person's ministry. God's timetable of ministry revolves around our growth and maturity in Him and our willingness to allow Him to be Lord in every area of our lives.

Receive God's Promise in Faith The Scriptures show us that people of God have missed God's best for them by not receiving His Word in faith. Hebrews 4:2 says, "For indeed the good news came to us just as to them; but the message they heard did not benefit them, because they were not united by faith with those who listened."

While the accomplishment of any prophetic directive is largely up to God, our role in the process is to put aside doubt, and to give God freedom to make whatever changes in us that are necessary to bring about His plan.

"If you have received personal prophecies from the Lord, or your church has received prophetic words, go back and read over them again. If you've neglected them, repent and commit yourself to responding in faith instead."

"What has the Lord said to you? Begin to say it with Him. Confess it to yourself and to others. Once you've started confessing God's word to you, it's time to act on it as well. Take those refresher lessons for that instrument God said you will use in worship. Start that Bible correspondence course to prepare yourself for the mission field. Set aside the money you'll be needing to make it all come to pass. Get ready to see God's prophetic word bear fruit."

"Finally, flow with the authority God has placed over you and in you, and join with others to exercise corporate faith—both for the words given to you and for the words given to the whole congregation."

Peter declared in Acts 2:17 that the prophet Joel was speaking of the Church age when he proclaimed, "I will pour out my Spirit in those days, and your sons and daughters shall prophesy."

In 1 Corinthians 14:39, 40 the apostle Paul writes, "Therefore, brethren, desire earnestly to prophesy, and do not forbid to speak with tongues. Let all things be done decently and in order." The Greek word used in this passage for covet or desire earnestly is Zeloo, which means to have great desire, to be jealous over and to be zealously affected. This term notes a fervency of mind and emotional jealousy, as a husband would be jealous for his wife. The only divine attributes that the church is told to covet are the gifts of the spirit.

The reason that God calls for us to covet the gifts, especially prophecy, is that these manifestations are not for our own benefit, but primarily for the benefit of others. It takes an unselfish, dedicated Christian to be raised in purity and maturity in their ministry.

The Gifts of the Spirit are a manifestation of God's love and grace. God continues to reveal Himself to individuals and groups of Christians in the Church today to mature them and to bring about His plan and His Kingdom in the Earth.

He wants you to eagerly desire to be used in the gift of personal prophecy so that He can make Himself known to lost and hurting people through you. What a privilege it is to be His minister of reconciliation to his lost sheep (2 Corinthians 5:18-20). We are His ambassadors in the earth today. He desires for believers to walk in the manifestation of the Holy Spirit to see the Great Commission fulfilled so that those who are lost in darkness can come to know Him as their Father.

Now is the time to "let all things be done, decently and in order"!

To help bring Christians into a place of maturity, God has set within the Church the ministry of the New Testament prophet with special anointing and authority. Through the manifestation of the Holy Spirit, He has also established the gift of prophecy to communicate in the local church. And as He inhabits the praises and prayer times of His people, He releases the spirit of prophecy to give testimony to the Lordship of Jesus Christ in the earth today!

The Bible makes it clear that prophecy is the most powerful gift, and it is encouraged throughout the Scriptures.

The apostle Paul spoke of the proper biblical response to personal prophecy in his letter to the Corinthians:

So, dear brothers and sisters, be eager to prophesy, and don't forbid speaking in tongues. But be sure that everything is done properly and in order (1 Corinthians 14:39-40).

The Bible provides us with general guidelines to help us properly respond to personal prophecy.

1. Does the word line up with Scripture?

Someone may say to you, "I've had a vision about your life," or "The Lord has given me this great word for you." God does lead supernaturally, there is no doubt about it. But whenever you are considering any form of special guidance, you need to judge it against the light of God's Word to see if it is true. The apostle Paul gave the litmus test for prophets in his first letter to the Thessalonians: Do not stifle the Holy Spirit. Do not scoff at prophecies, but test everything that is said. Hold on to what is good (1 Thessalonians 5:19-21).

In every prophetic word you should ask, does the prophecy line up with the Bible? The Holy Spirit will never act in contradiction to the written Word of God. He is the One who inspired the Bible in the first place.

Christians should know the Bible and memorize key portions of it. It is the Word of God that will protect us against false doctrine, deception, and spiritual manipulation. Always check a prophetic word against the other seven keys, beginning with the Bible. If the prophecy contradicts the Scriptures, you can obviously ignore it.

2. What is the character and fruit of the person giving the word?

The personal character of a prophetic minister, or any minister for that matter, is the foundation of his or her ministry. Character is a primary guide for determining whether someone is a true or false prophet.

3. Is the prophecy given in love and grace, or in anger and judgment?

Prophecy in the New Testament flows from the Spirit of Christ, which is a spirit of grace and love. As we have already considered, the majority of personal prophecy should be given as edification, exhortation, and comfort (1 Corinthians 14:3).

It is interesting that the portion of Scripture that has become known as the "love chapter," 1 Corinthians 13, is sandwiched between the two chapters that deal with the manifestation of the Holy Spirit. Through these gifts God shows His love to the world, and He expects His ministers to do the same.

4. Is there some sort of religious bias in the attitude of the person giving the word?

Sometimes a person will bring what could be termed a doctrinal "hobby horse" into a prophetic situation that can twist a true prophecy and give it an unbalanced presentation. Be careful to judge the word against the Bible, and not against the position of a certain denomination or religious group.

5. Do I sense a witness from the Holy Spirit?

When a guitarist tunes his guitar, he will play one note and then match the next string on the guitar to the note on the first string. A true musician can hear the discord when their instrument is out of tune, and they will tinker with the tuning key until there is tone between the two strings.

Objects have certain characteristic frequencies at which they vibrate. If you cause one object (for instance a bell) to vibrate near another object with the same characteristic frequency (another bell of the same size and weight and shape), the second object will begin to vibrate by itself. That is something like what happens when we hear the voice of the Lord—we resonate.

When the Lord is speaking to us, no matter what method He chooses, our born-again spirits recognize the voice of the Good Shepherd. Jesus made it clear in John 10 that His sheep know His voice, and the voice of a stranger they will not follow. If a personal prophecy is not of God, the born-again Christian will get what is known as a "check" in their spirit—an uncomfortable feeling in the pit of the stomach telling them that something is not right.

6. Don't reject a directional word, but test it against the other keys.

If the word is something new that you have never heard before, it may be a directional word from the Lord, but don't act on it right away. Test it like you would any other guidance from the Lord.

Remember, personal prophecy is only one of the seven keys of God's guidance, and it alone should not be leaned on in making major decisions in our life. However, it is an important way that God guides the New Testament believer, and it should not be overlooked in seeking God's direction for our lives.

Share your thoughts: How has personal prophecy affected your life?

HOLY PROPHECY

If God heals our mind, we are still in danger
1. We could relapse
2. Our spirit could still be dead to God.

When God comes to take us to heaven, we would NOT be ready. Today's prophets are warning that our time is short. The urgency is not only to be healed in mind and body, but also in spirit. We need to be so well, that we ourselves operate daily in the power of Jesu s Christ, healing, raising the dead, and fixing the immediate need, based on God's will.

Prophecy is knowing plus sharing—the mind of Christ, the thoughts of men, the secrets of men, the cause of illnesses, and/or the future. A true prophecy always comes true if we line up with it. A true prophet will never take God's credit. Rather he/she will always deflect/give all glory to God.

WHY WE NEED PROPHETIC MINISTRY

The foundation of prophetic ministry is important. Why does the modern-day church need prophetic ministry? We live in increasingly difficult and complex times; therefore it becomes imperative to hear God's voice clearly. God wants to protect His children. We need to hear His voice when He warns us of dangerous situations to prepare for or to avoid. As the world around us becomes increasingly shaky, Christians will need to depend more and more on God and His leading for their very survival. God uses the prophetic to direct and protect His people. God uses prophecy to warn us about upcoming disasters and prepares the church for future needs. Therefore, it becomes important for the church to acknowledge the validity of prophetic ministry and to take it seriously.

Even though God has given us His Word, the Bible does not cover every situation in our lives. That's why we have also received the Holy Spirit so we have the ability to hear God about situations not outlined in His Word. In addition to the Holy Spirit speaking to us directly, God also uses prophets to make His will known to His church. The place of the prophetic ministry is to equip the saints so they know God's voice and follow His leading.

THE HEART OF THE PROPHETIC PERSON

God looks at what is in our hearts because that's where truth is found. We need to constantly evaluate our motives and our actions, so that they truly represent God's heart instead of our own selfish will. And the only way to know God's heart is to establish an intimate relationship with Him. That relationship is the basic foundation of a prophetic ministry, and it also brings a friendship with God. The prophets are God's friends.

If we want to be used in prophetic ministry, we must be "open" to God so He can use us. But that is not enough. The Bible instructs us to seek the gifts of the Spirit, especially the gift of prophecy. And our primary motivation to operate in this gift must be to act in love. God's purposes can be accomplished only when we move and act in Christ's love.

There are mistakes that have been made in the application of the prophetic. However, we must move past the mistakes, not throwing out prophecy; we must learn from our mistakes. I feel that one key to a well functioning prophetic ministry is to be able to receive, interpretation and judge prophetic revelation correctly.

A prophet is also a friend of God. He has established such an intimate relationship with God that God delights in revealing His plans to him. This relationship also entails the fear of the Lord, which isn't like the fear of men. If we are to speak the true words of God, we must be delivered from the fear of men. It comes with the understanding that God wil l choose various ways through which He will flow through His vessels. It restricts God's ability to use us in the way He may want when we copy another prophet. Jesus is the one we need to copy, not men and not other prophetic ministries. God wants the special gifts He has given to us to flow freely and efficiently through us.

It is also important to understand that we're not necessarily called to the office of prophet simply because we flow in a prophetic gifting.

People will sometimes make mistakes when they move in the prophetic. We shouldn't disqualify that person or call him a fal se prophet simply because he makes a mistake. If we put our confidence in our own abilities, we set ourselves up for failure. Our confidence should rest only on God's ability, not our own. That mindset allows God to work through His vessels more efficiently and accomplish His purposes in advancing the kingdom.

REJECTION AND PRIDE ISSUES

Some people are concerned that they will be rejected if they allow God to manifest His supernatural power through them. Fear of rejection can keep people from moving in the prophetic. Most of us have experienced rejection—and rejection is part of any true ministry. We have to die to self so rejection doesn't have power over us. Those who are still affected by rejection haven't completed the dying-to-self process. When we are rejected, we have an opportunity to demonstrate God's love and power to those who reject us. God will use our experiences of rejection to work Christ-likeness and spiritual maturity in us.

We must allow God's forgiveness to bring healing to our rejection wounds, or those wounds will influence the way we minister to God's people. These wounds can possibly corrupt the ministry because we will base our response on the rejection, bitterness and hurts we have received instead of on the love of God. The interesting part is that once we've healed from our wounds, we will receive authority in the very place we were wounded. God uses every trial to prepare us so we may grow in spiritual authority and thereby minister to those who are going through the same situations and trials.

We must watch our motives if we want to walk with God in true spiritual authority. If our motive is to promote our agendas and ministries, then our ministry isn't grounded in God. We need a personal and intimate relationship with God before He can establish us in a prophetic ministry. That relationship enables us to seek His approval instead of looking for approval from people. And if G od has truly called us into ministry, we must let Him put us into the position in His timing instead of striving to do it our way. That means we may not accept opportunities offered to us if they are not in God's timing or brought about by Him. Instead, we make it our goal to walk in humility before God (Psalms 15:33).

We never use the prophetic to manipulate and control, for that would be witchcraft. Rather, prophecy is a ministry that functions in unity. Our eyes need to be focused solely on the Lord and the eyes of our hearts need opened so we may know the hope to which He has called us (Ephesians 1:18). Our perspective determines how we will interpret prophetic revelation, therefore it is important for us to use God's perspective, w hich is an eternal perspective. God's perspective is also a perspective of potential, and we must operate in that vision of God's potential when we move in the prophetic. This type of vision allows us to see life even in something that seems dead.

TRUE AND COUNTERFEIT PROPHETS

There is no doubt that there are counterfeit prophets. Think about this, copies can be made only from originals. In other words, if there weren't real prophets, there wouldn't be counterfeit ones. The Lord allows the tares to help His people be prepared for the "ultimate last-day confrontation." Matthew 13:30 points out the dangers of prematurely uprooting the tares: "Allow both to grow together until the harvest." Often developing prophets, who are just beginning to walk in this ministry, make mistakes and may be perceived as false prophets when they aren't. They're just learning and should be allowed the time to grow into the gifting God has given them. Removing them prematurely from the field will be more destructive than helpful.

Sometimes God uses controversy to bring purity into the ministry He is raising up and developing. Controversy results in evaluation, evaluation causes adjustments to be made. And it reveals those who may be in the ministry out of selfish ambition. There does come a time when the wheat needs to be separate d from the tares so "bread can be made from it." But we must not be premature in doing that separation.

COMMON STUMBLING BLOCKS

There are various stumbling blocks that will keep us from moving in the fullness of a prophetic ministry.

These include:
to be tempted to use standard formulas that are outlined in various books that teach about prophetic symbolism when interpreting visions and revelations.

Looking only from our personal, present perspective, We must interpret revelations not from our perspective, but from God's eternal perspective. If we interpret all revelations using the same formula, we will get inaccurate interpretations.

Seeing through fear rather than faith, We're not to interpret prophecy through fear, but rather through faith. Fear is also based in suspicion and suspicion will never result in accurate interpretation. True discernment operates only in true godly love.

Majoring on minors, The importance of preparing the way for the King and not primarily focusing on what the enemy is doing.

Prejudices, When we prophesy we should guard against prejudice because prejudice can seriously distort a revelation and the actual meaning of it.

Having prejudicial doctrines, Prophecy isn't meant to establish doctrines. That has already been established through the Bible.

Rejection, Dwelling on rejection will keep us self-centered, which will distort the meaning of the revelations God is giving us as well.

Bitterness, The possible result of unhealed wounds that make us sensitive in those areas.

Rebellion, The refusal to submit to authority rooted in either rejection or self-will.

Unsanctified mercy, Having mercy about situations the Lord may be using to judge or bring correction. The important thing is to be ruled by the Holy Spirit and to gain an understanding of what God is doing. When we move in human compassion we may be tempted to take on burdens the Lord hasn't given us in the first place.

The "party spirit", The temptation to believe that our ministry is the most important one and the lack of understanding that God uses all ministries to work together as one.

Failing to submit to the body, God intentionally does not reveal everything to just one ministry, but reveals parts of visions and revelations to various ministries. He does that so that one ministry will depend on others, and a working together to understand the entire picture is essential.

Lust, "One of the primary destroyers of prophetic vision." We need to put a guard on our eyes so our eyes are single and thereby the entire body can be full of God's light. In this way we won't use our eyes for evil.

Using natural eyes instead of the "eye of our heart", We must understand that the things of God must be interpreted by the Spirit and not by our own perspectives and reasoning.

Our words speak either life or death. As we grow in the prophetic and in our relationship with God we will find more and more that there is power in our words especially when God puts His anointing on them. A word spoken within the right timing and God's anointing is very powerful. It is important that we abide in the Word itself for God uses His Word to express Himself in His language. We learn the spiritual (symbolic) language through dreams and visions. Like many things, it requires time and patience to produce lasting fruit. A problem won't be eliminated by dealing with the symptoms. Instead we must put the ax to the root of the problem tree—deal with the source and thereby also remove the symptoms. The Lord works a deep work from the inside out, not the outside in. It's that type of working that will create deep and lasting changes.

God is a practical God and His fruit is a practical fruit. It needs to be our goal to not just bear fruit, but to bear fruit that lasts. It requires patience to bear lasting fruit. But it's worth the wait because when there is lasting fruit, Christ will be lifted up by His people and "all men will be drawn to Him."

GOD SPEAKS TO US THROUGH HIS WORD

One of the greatest tools is God's written Word. In it we learn about His character, His likes and dislikes, His promises and His standards. The more we become familiar with the Word of God, the easier it is to distinguish between the voices we hear. In this process we must acknowledge God's Word as the absolute standard of truth. God will never go against His written Word, the Bible. So if we think we have heard Him say something to us that contradicts Scripture, we must assume we have heard wrong.

There are times when we are in desperate situations and feel the need for an immediate response from God. In our desperation we may search the Scriptures for a word that fits our situation and then interpret it in a way that agrees with our desires. This is an example of misusing Scriptures. There are two types of misuses:

Manipulating scripture—When we are desperate for a word, we may be tempted to find a Scripture we think fits our situation, then twist it to fit our purposes. We can end up trying to hold God to a promise He never made, and then be disappointed when He doesn't keep that "promise."

Using the Bible out of context—Some people use Scripture like a spiritual horoscope—they open the Bible and randomly select a Scripture, accepting that Scripture as the answer to their situation. There are times when God will speak to us by having us randomly come across a Scripture, but that is the exception rather than the norm.

DOING WHAT WE HEAR GOD SAY

The main issue is not determining what God wants to say to us; the hard part is obeying Him after we hear Him. It is not easy to "walk out God's will once we understand it." If you want to hear God clearly, you must be prepared to obey Him once you have heard Him.

KNOWING IT IS REALLY GOD

So how do we know it is really God? When we are not sure, we can ask Him. But we must allow Him to decide how to confirm it to us. We are not in a place to dictate to God how and when He will confirm His will to us. In fact, we are told in the Bible not to put the Lord to the test, e.g. do not fleece God. It is better to simply leave the question for clarification with the Lord and let Him decide when and how He will answer it.

Many of us have the tendency to over analyze revelations. While we spend too much time trying to make sure it is God, the opportunity passes and we miss God's perfect timing and deliver the message in the wrong season. This happens when we put our trust in our abilities and not God's. It is important to put our trust solely in the Lord and His willingness to redirect us if need be. Often we assume that a message pertains to the present time and discard it because it may not fit into a current situation. It does not mean that a word is not from God if it does not happen to "fit" your current situations. He may be dealing with something that will happen tomorrow or next month. It is always good to ask the Lord to clarify the timing of a word.

In trying to learn God's voice, it is equally important to know what is not God's voice. There are several keys to distinguishing what is and is not God's voice:

God never contradicts His Word. When we receive a word that states something different from Scripture, it is safe to toss it out.

God's voice never is the voice of anxiety, unsettledness nor exhaustion. When our emotions are highly involved it is best to wait until God's peace is settled in us.

God's voice is not the voice of obscurity. He does not make His communication to us difficult by giving us difficult riddles and symbols to identify.

God is not a gossip and will not reveal anything about a person to us unless we are part of the problem or part of the solution. This means that we may be given an assignment to pray for somebody and God strategically reveals how to pray for that person by revealing the source of the issue or He may want us to help that person in a physical manner, i.e. helping them financially or providing support to them.

God's voice does not condemn. God wants His children to learn and He lovingly corrects while providing a way for improvement.

DEFINING PROPHECY

Many questions about prophecy and the prophetic ministry abound. But what is prophecy? Thompson defines prophecy as "speaking divine encouragement" as well as "hearing from God and speaking what you hear in order to build, comfort, or encourage someone." God gives us spiritual gifts through which he manifests prophecy.

1 Corinthians 12:8-10 states: "To one there is given through the Spirit the message of wisdom, to another the message of knowledge by means of the same Spirit, to another faith by the same Spirit, to another gifts of healing, by that one Spirit, to another miraculous powers, to another prophecy, to another distinguishing between spirits, to another speaking in different kinds of tongues, and to still another interpretation of tongues." Three of the gifts listed in 1 Corinthians 12:8-10 are revelatory. These are words of knowledge, words of wisdom and discerning the spirits.

A word of knowledge is knowledge of a specific fact about a person, place or event that was not obtained through natural means. A word of wisdom is a divine revelation of the will, plan or purpose of God for a specific situation. And discerning of spirits is the ability to recognize and distinguish between types of spirits and anointings. Thompson states: "Words of knowledge, words of wisdom and discerning of spirits are gifts in the same way that guns, ammunition, and grenades are gifts for a soldier. They are divine empowerments to operate in the supernatural revelation and power of God."

It is important to understand that receiving a revelation is only part of a prophecy. An impression from the Lord would be useless if we don't know what to do with it or how to interpret it. This is why we need to understand prophecy in three parts: revelation, interpretation and application.

INTERPRETATION

Interpretation is the stage of a revelation where most of the mistakes are made. The key to effective interpretation is to have a close relationship with God and to know His Word. By doing so, we learn about His character and the things He likes and dislikes and should thereby be quick to recognize whether a source is of God.

Thompson writes: "Interpretations are often derived through an interplay between our understanding of interpretative principles, our sensitivity to the Holy Spirit, and our heart attitude. To accurately interpret God's mind, we must also possess His heart."

There are four hindrances that may cause us to misinterpret a revelation. These are opinions, offenses and bitterness, sin and spiritual bondages as well as carnal judgment.

Opinions—We must have the mind of the Lord and not rely on our own opinions. For example, "pet doctrines" are a dangerous type of opinion. Such doctrines are religiously motivated and may be given a position of false importance.

Offenses and bitterness—This happens when we have not forgiven those who have offended us. By doing so, an offense can become established in our heart and when we interpret a revelation we will interpret it through those offenses. Any negative revelation about somebody or a group of people we are offended by, should be suspect. It is vital to our prophetic effectiveness that we walk in forgiveness.

Sin and spiritual bondages—When we have unconfessed sin in our lives, we are allowing a stronghold that will prevent us from accurately interpreting a revelation. Such strongholds include lust, bitterness, rebellion or a religious spirit.

Carnal judgment—This is when we judge people by their outward appearances.

RESPONDING TO PROPHECY

Anyone can receive a prophecy but responding is a big part in bringing that finished promise God has for you. A truly inspired personal prophecy is God's specific word to an individual.

Several attitudes are critical for receiving a personal prophecy properly: Faith is absolutely essential for receiving anything from God. If we intend to receive personal prophecy from a prophetic person or a prophet, we should evaluate fully those who might minister prophetically to us. If we conclude that they are qualified, competent men and women of God, then the prophecies should be received in confidence, believing that word to be true and factual.

If the gospel, which is the power of God, could not profit, how much more so is that true when a prophet of today speaks a word from the Lord.

If a prophetic word is received with an attitude of acceptance and faith, when it is heard it will create faith for the fulfillment of that word: "So then faith cometh by hearing, and hearing by the word of God" (Romans 10:17). Faith is the purchaser of all God's prophetic promises. Without faith it is impossible to please God, but with faith in God all things are possible (Hebrews 11:6; Mark 9:23; I John 5:4). True faith will be accompanied by the work of obedience. If our hearing does not advance to the point of our doing, we become a candidate for deception, "Be ye doers of the word, and not hearers only, deceiving your own selves" (James 1:22). The Lord speaks a prophetic word to us, not just to tickle our mind, but to bring the understanding necessary to do the will of God: "Those things which are revealed belong unto us and to our children forever, that we may do all the words of this law" (Deuteronomy. 29:29). It is better not to receive a word at all than to receive one and then not do what the word says to do. But if we obey and do exactly what the Word says, then we deliver ourselves from deception and open our spirit and mind to know the will of God. So if we believe and do what we know to do, Christ will speak and reveal more concerning His Will and plan. The proper response to personal prophecy requires obedience, a co-operation with the word that allows it to have room in our lives for the fulfillment of God's will. After we have received a personal prophecy, and proven it to be a true word from the Lord, we must maintain a constant faith and confidence that it will come to pass regardless of the time required and that requires patiently pursuing God's will. We must allow no one to rob us of our personal prophecies. In the past discouragement came because nothing was happening as quickly as I had expected. I just wanted to give up. But thank God they were not destroyed, for everyone of them has come to pass. They have been a constant source of inspiration, encouragement, and motivation over the last twenty years.

Personal Prophecies Are Precious. The devil can use well-meaning ministers and Christian friends to rob us of our word from the Lord, but we must not let them. Our personal prophecies may presently be causing us confusion and frustration. They may be discouraging because what was promised is not happening in the time and way we think it should. They may contradict everything that is now in our life and circumstances. We must wait patiently upon the Lord, and He will fulfill His prophetic word, changing both us and our circumstances. If we press on patiently pursuing our Word from the Lord, we will eventually possess all our prophetic promises. Every true word from God will come to pass in His predestined purpose and timing. God's process for prophetic fulfillment is rarely sooner than we expect. It is almost always later, and sometimes much later. I say something all the time "God is never early but He is always on time. When I was first ordained I expected to be launched into worldwide ministry because of the prophecies over me. I expected all those glowing words about being "a leader of leaders" to become an instant reality. Having been given a promise of "the gifts of the Spirit and the faith of God, the ministry of deliverance and anointing to bring the Body of Christ together, and prophetic anointing," I fully believed they would be manifested immediately. To be honest most of my prophetic promises was a twenty year adventure. Wrong Perception Brings Pressure and Impatience. Many other ministers like me were convinced that Jesus was coming any moment. We had no time to waste. I definitely believed that Jesus would return before now. We could only think in terms of months, not years. Waiting and patience was not part of our vocabulary then; everything had to be done today because there was not going to be a tomorrow. God is never in a hurry, but He is always on time. God is not motivated by intimidation or frustration. In my life I was a minister within the Church and used for any and all types of ministry. God was making the man before He could manifest the ministry fully. As with all of us, the ministry could be no greater than the man. If it were, the immature man would be destroyed, because we must be properly prepared to carry the full weight of mature ministry.

Even with Jesus, God took thirty years of life on earth for preparation, and only three for ministry a ten to one ratio. Waiting upon the Lord for our prophecies to come to pass demonstrates not only patience, but also faith and obedience.

When we receive a true word of prophecy and respond with religion, pride, anger, doubt, resentment, criticism, self-justification, or arrogance, we reveal immaturity or a wrong spirit. The result is that our attitude neutralizes much of what God wants to accomplish by the words spoken. For that reason, it is critical that we receive the prophetic utterance in a spirit of humility. Sometimes we have a preconceived idea about a great ministry we believe God will confirm and describe through the prophet. When God does not confirm our ideas of great self-importance, then we may become disillusioned, depressed, and angry at God and the one prophesying. We insist that the prophet or prophetic person has missed the mind of God.

A mature person with the right attitude will respond to personal prophecy even if it is corrective with the attributes of heavenly wisdom. A righteous and mature person will not respond with carnal or childish behavior even if a prophecy is inaccurate. How much more should we then, respond to a true personal prophecy with humility. Pride Can Hinder Personal Prophecy From Coming to Pass. Nothing can stop the Word from working once we have obeyed in every detail. We do not have to beg God to make it work. Obedience to a prophecy activates it into fulfillment as surely as the right key opens the door.

PROPHETIC LANGUAGE

You may have noticed that a husband and wife may be able to communicate in an unusual language. Most may not understand it but the couple does. The same is true of our relationship to God. The longer we know Him and the more intimately acquainted we become with Him, the better we are able to understand His words to us and respond to them appropriately. Understanding God's words to us is not as easy as it may seem at first. So we must get to know God's prophetic language.

Though God never seems to be in a hurry, He is always on time. But He often seems to take longer than we think He should. Some of the greatest failures of the Bible resulted from their impatience with God as they waited for a prophecy to be fulfilled. Whenever we jump ahead of God's agenda for prophetic fulfillment, we always produce something in the flesh that eventually opposes the fruit of the true prophetic promise. If God has spoken a clear prophetic promise to you, He will come through in time His time. He will either be there in time to rescue the situation, or He will resurrect it to live again. Knowing that God has His own time schedule can be an encouragement to those who are walking by faith while believing in God's faithfulness to bring forth His prophetic promise. But it can also be a frustration to the flesh, trying the patience of the saints. His schedule may not always make sense to the natural man's reasoning. But I have learned, that His timetable is necessary for fullness, maturity, and bringing everything together in proper order.

When God uses the Word "immediately", we want it now! On the surface, it may seem that a sudden event has happened spontaneously. "Suddenly" on the day of Pentecost they all began to speak with other tongues as they were baptized with the Holy Spirit. But this came about according to God's timetable, and man's preparation and placement. It may seem as though no one, not even God, will ever recognize, receive, and support the vision or ministry. But suddenly, when it has reached full maturity, when the person, the ministry, and God's purpose are ready, then immediately God harvests it by bringing it into full activity and fulfillment. It is then mightily manifested to the Church and the world. Therefore, we should not worry about when God will move to fulfill the vision and manifest the ministry He has given us.

In prophetic Language, however, these terms do not always have their everyday meaning. God's prophetic timetable, "now" may be years later. Because of this principle of prophetic language, it is sometimes difficult to determine whether a personal prophecy is speaking of things past, present or future. Based on Biblical examples and my own many years of experience, however, I have found the following timetable for prophetic language to be helpful, but not severe: Immediately means from one day to five years. Very soon means one to ten years. Now or this day means one to forty years. I will without a definite time designation means God will act sometime in the person's life if he is obedient. Soon was the word Jesus used to describe the time of His soon return almost two thousand years ago.

When God says prophetically that He will give us wisdom that means He will allow some problems and situations to arise which are beyond our capacity to solve. They will force us to draw on God's wisdom, giving Him an opportunity to fulfill His promise. After all, we really have no need of divine wisdom unless all sources of human wisdom have been worn out and proven insufficient to solve a problem.

When we are told in prophecy that we will have great faith, we should realize that the soil of the fruit of faith is life on the brink of disaster in need of a miracle. If we never are put in a position by God where we cannot meet our own needs by our own means, then we will never grow the fruit of faith. I have prophesied to people about them getting a new job or even a promotion. The next time I see them they tell me they got fired. It was hard to understand but we have to lose something to get the something new God is speaking.

If we truly believe God's personal prophetic promise to us concerning a great ministry, then, we must start now to co-operate with the word so we will be ready for its fulfillment in due season. By faith we must begin our preparation, practicing patiently until the promise is accomplished. If we do not have faith to prepare ourselves even when no ministry opportunity is in sight, or when we fail to see how it can become a reality, we will miss our opportunity to participate in the promise. Sometimes the preparation process will not make any sense to our natural reasoning. But if we prepare anyway, God will provide abundantly according to His prophetic word.

If we hear that a great victory is coming, but we are not currently fighting a battle, then we need to be prepared for one. We cannot have a great victory without a great battle; little battles bring only little victories. So whenever we hear words like "victory, overcome or triumph we can be assured of a fight. But we can also be confident of victory.

GIFTS AND CALLING

How do we come to know our calling, gifts or ministry anointing? God may give you dreams, visions, supernatural manifestations, prophetic voice, angelic visitation or even a highlight of scripture. In the Bible days the Apostles laid their hands on and released prophetic presbytery.

God doesn't limit Himself to one way to call us. It is amazing how God will call you. I believe that there are no two calls alike. If you look at our bodies, we will see no two arms or two legs alike. They are similar but different. We do need to know our five fold ministry but I've seen people get so consumed with it that they are more focused on position than God.

God called me from my childhood. But the biggest portion of my call came about 1988-1990. God said I would study His Word to show myself approved and miracles, signs and wonders will follow you. This has all been fulfilled and was not anything I could see at that time. Now today I now have prophesied to well over a thousand people, seen miracles in the many.

It is time to activate your ministry and personal prophecies. Personal prophecy directed by the Holy Spirit that God is speaking to you. When God speaks something, it is decreed in Heaven. You become pregnant with God's plans and carry it until it's time to be birthed.

The prophetic Word is like a seed that has been planted by God and He watches over it to watch it grow. The anointing that flows with a prophetic Word is like the necessary ingredient of yeast that makes bread grow. Ministry can be activated by personal prophecy and the anointing.

Any ministry will not work by self appointing yourself. God spoke to me once and said that no one can send themselves. He said if a person gets into the envelope to be sent they need someone to lick the envelope to seal it.

There are always those who try to produce their ministry without discipline. Any substitute is a counterfeit. If we produce a ministry without the leading of God it will be more of a hurt than a help.

I can truly say that the greatest increase of my call came through impartation.

1 Timothy 4:14 Neglect not the gift that is in thee, which was given thee by prophecy, with the laying on of the hands of the presbytery.

2 Timothy 1:6 Wherefore I put thee in remembrance that thou stir up the gift of God, which is in thee by the putting on of my hands.

Impartation can cause a similar release of the same anointing and power in a person's life. We need to receive impartation from those we can be sure are right in their hearts. I have said this for years that there is more caught than taught. When you sit under mighty men or women of God you will catch some impartation. The laying on of hands though does release much more.

OUR RESPONSE

The Bible indicates that we are not to despise prophecy.

1 Thessalonians 5:20, 21 Despise not prophesyings. Prove all things; hold fast that which is good.

1 Corinthians 12:31 But covet earnestly the best gifts: and yet shew I unto you a more excellent way.

1 Corinthians 14:1 Follow after charity, and desire spiritual *gifts,* but rather that ye may prophesy.

1 Corinthians 14:39 Wherefore brethren, covet to prophesy, and forbid not to speak with tongues.

I am one that believes the anointing on the office of the prophet is for even more. Prophets are able to give direction, instruction, correction, motivation and deal with areas of a person's life personally.

When a prophet speaks to you with out knowing you, it is the best feeling of the love of God. I have seen hundreds of the most hopeless and depressed people time and time again healed by the power of God. When the personal Word is being released and the tears begin to flow down it causes the person to feel that they are loved and not forsaken.

Galatians 5:22 But the fruit of the Spirit is love, joy, peace, longsuffering, gentleness, goodness, faith,

Prophecy makes God's love more real and brings a peace beyond any other type of counsel or ministry. Prophecy to activate hope and even to remove shame.

The presence of God and the Word of God delivered will bring conviction to us concerning sin.

A personal prophecy can be concerning a great ministry, miracles or some of the anointings to be stirred up for the full call upon our lives.

One thing that I want to get into here is when a prophet speaks to you it always should be in love. Even if we are corrected the Word will come in love.

Many of the Body of Christ today leave no room for error in those who prophesy. Let me tell you even the most accurate of prophets can make a mistake of interpretation. The one thing we have to remember though is if we receive a prophecy that was a mistake that doesn't make the person a false prophet. Prophet is to be a gift to the Church. There are false prophets but not being accurate is not what makes them a false prophet. If you want to learn more read my book "Defeating the Demonic Realm" because it has the characteristics of false prophets. There are more true prophets than false. I know many whom have made mistakes but I know that the office of the prophet is under much attack and it can take a toll on their anointing and ability. This is why we should never judge someone as false when they just have made a mistake.

One thing that may shock you is there are many Christians operating in witchcraft prophecy. When anyone uses prayer or prophecy to control others according to their own will rather than God's will they are guilty of the sin of witchcraft. God is not the one who answers witchcraft prayers or prophecies. Satan is the source of witchcraft in any form. These are fiery darts aimed at children of God. Well meaning Christians have used witchcraft prayers to try to stop other churches and children of God. If you find yourself being prayed or prophesied against in this way for the purpose of selfish manipulation, do not respond the same way. At the end of the Litchfield Revival I faced extreme witchcraft attacks. God gave me some key scriptures and I will list them below.

Matthew 5:44 But I say unto you, Love your enemies, bless them that curse you, do good to them that hate you, and pray for them which despitefully use you, and persecute you;

Luke 6:28 Bless them that curse you, and pray for them which despitefully use you.

Romans 12:14 Bless them which persecute you: bless, and curse not.

1 Corinthians 4:12 And labour, working with our own hands: being reviled, we bless; being persecuted, we suffer it:

There cannot be counterfeit prophecies unless there are God's true prophecies. When you find real prophets and receive the benefits of true prophecies. Remember we are to despise not prophesying.

PROPHETIC PERSONALITY

Everyone seems to want a prophetic Word but we need to understand God's personal way that never changes. The first one I want to talk about is we prophesy in part.

1 Corinthians 13:9 For we know in part, and we prophesy in part.

God only reveals what we need to know for the time and place. The Word of God will only cover a portion of God's plan for us. God will speak about our ultimate ministry and will not tell us about the trials or other ministry until that ultimate ministry takes place.

We need to understand prophecy always reveals only a part of God's Word to us. Many times that piece of God's puzzle you want to hear from God will not be the part you want to hear many times.

While God does release part of His plans through the prophetic Words, His Word also unfolds with increase. It unfolds and expands over the years, adding new information and revelation. God will slowly reveal His full plan for our lives and the resources for bringing them to pass.

One of the most important things that most Christians don't remember is prophecies are conditional. We may receive a Word from God and depending on our behavior it may not come to pass because of our decisions. Conditional prophecies are Words from God that can be altered or reversed. They may fail and never be fulfilled. The one whom spoke the Word will have released a sure Word from God but there were conditions not followed. If you have a contract in business there may be conditions that must be followed or the contract becomes void. The same thing happens with the prophetic Word.

Listen, ALL prophecies are conditional whether or not any were spoken. Conditional prophecy depends on obedience. Prophecy will be based on our attitude, and our actions are the conditions for the fulfillment of our personal prophecy. You may have to pass a series of tests over the years like Abraham that will allow God's purpose to come to pass. Sin will void out your prophetic fulfillment.

1 Samuel 15:22 And Samuel said, Hath the LORD *as great* delight in burnt offerings and sacrifices, as in obeying the voice of the LORD? Behold, to obey *is* better than sacrifice, *and* to hearken than the fat of rams.

Prophecy requires faith and obedience.

Hebrews 3:7-17 Wherefore (as the Holy Ghost saith, To day if ye will hear his voice, Harden not your hearts, as in the provocation, in the day of temptation in the wilderness: When your fathers tempted me, proved me, and saw my works forty years. Wherefore I was grieved with that generation, and said, They do alway err in *their* heart; and they have not known my ways. So I sware in my wrath, They shall not enter into my rest.) Take heed, brethren, lest there be in any of you an e vil heart of unbelief, in departing from the living God. But exhort one another daily, while it is called To day; lest any of you be hardened through the deceitfulness of sin. For we are made partakers of Christ, if we hold the beginning of our confidence stedfast unto the end; While it is said, To day if ye will hear his voice, harden not your hearts, as in the provocation. For some, when they had heard, did provoke: howbeit not all that came out of Egypt by Moses. But with whom was he grieved forty years? *was it* not with them that had sinned, whose carcases fell in the wilderness?

Hebrews 4:1, 2 Let us therefore fear, lest, a promise being left *us* of entering into his rest, any of you should seem to come short of it. For unto us was the gospel preached, as well as unto them: but the word preached did not profit them, not being mixed with faith in them that heard *it*.

We need to learn from all those in the Bible whom fell short of fulfilling their prophecy. When you receive the partial plan through prophecy and see God's progressive plan unfold you must remember that there will be conditions in them being fulfilled.

PROPHETIC MOUTHPIECE

A prophetic Word can be delivered in many forms. I believe God can speak in many ways so let's not close our minds to any of them.

THE OFFICE OF THE PROPHET

Ephesians 2:20 And are built upon the foundation of the apostles and prophets, Jesus Christ himself being the chief corner *stone;*

Ephesians 4:11 And he gave some, apostles; and some, prophets; and some, evangelists; and some, pastors and teachers;

The Office of the prophet is a gift of the Holy Spirit to the Church. The Prophet is part of the foundation of the Body of Christ. The Prophet's have a heart for the Body of Christ. The Prophet received attributes of Christ that endowed Him with the ability to perceive what is in the heart of people, to proclaim God's plans and know the secrets of God. The Office of the Prophet is to function in a higher realm of ministry.

The office of the Prophet is anointed and has administrative authority. The prophet has authority to preach and prophesy. The purpose of the prophet is for the perfecting of the Saints.

1 Corinthians 12:28 And God hath set some in the church, first apostles, secondarily prophets, thirdly teachers, after that miracles, then gifts of healings, helps, governments, diversities of tongues.

Ephesians 2:20-22 And are built upon the foundation of the apostles and prophets, Jesus Christ himself being the chief corner *stone;* In whom all the building fitly framed together groweth unto an holy temple in the Lord: In whom ye also are builded together for an habitation of God through the Spirit.

It's time that Christ brings recognition to His prophets. God is restoring the fivefold ministry to the Church.

Prophets are anointed to know what is next of God's plan. This next number of prophets coming forth will prepare the way of Christ's return. These prophets shall gather and bring the Church into order to be without spot or wrinkle.

THE GIFT OF PROPHECY

Prophecy is one of the manifestations of the Holy Spirit. Prophecy is not given because of maturity. It's a GIFT.

Romans 12:6 Having then gifts differing according to the grace that is given to us, whether prophecy, *let us prophesy* according to the proportion of faith;

1 Thessalonians 5:20 Despise not prophesyings.

Acts 2:17 And it shall come to pass in the last days, saith God, I will pour out of my Spirit upon all flesh: and your sons and your daughters shall prophesy, and your young men shall see visions, and your old men shall dream dreams:

1 Corinthians 12:10 To another the working of miracles; to another prophecy; to another discerning of spirits; to another *divers* kinds of tongues; to another the interpretation of tongues:

1 Corinthians 14:1-6 Follow after charity, and desire spiritual *gifts,* but rather that ye may prophesy. For he that speaketh in an *unknown* tongue speaketh not unto men, but unto God: for no man understandeth *him;* howbeit in the spirit he speaketh mysteries. But he that prophesieth s peaketh unto men *to* edification, and exhortation, and comfort. He that speaketh in an *unknown* tongue edifieth himself; but he that prophesieth edifieth the church. I would that ye all spake with tongues, but rather that ye prophesied: for greater *is* he that prophesieth than he that speaketh with tongues, except he interpret, that the church may receive edifying. Now, brethren, if I come unto you speaking with tongues, what shall I profit you, except I shall speak to you either by revelation, or by knowledge, or by prophesying, or by doctrine?

1 Corinthians 14:22-24 Wherefore tongues are for a sign, not to them that believe, but to them that believe not: but prophesying *serveth* not for them that believe not, but for them which believe. If therefore the whole church be come together into one place, and all speak with tongues, and there come in *those that are* unlearned, or unbelievers, will they not say that ye are mad? But if all prophesy, and there come in one that believeth not, or *one* unlearned, he is convinced of all, he is judged of all:

1 Corinthians 14:31 For ye may all prophesy one by one, that all may learn, and all may be comforted.

1 Corinthians 14:39, 40 Wherefore, brethren, covet to prophesy, and forbid not to speak with tongues. Let all things be done decently and in order.

Any Christian can flow in the gifts of the Holy Spirit. There are many within the Body of Christ whom has a real gift of prophecy. The problem is there are too many who are in error. This is one of the main reasons I am writing the books like "Increasing Your Prophetic Gift & Receiving a Prophetic Word from God."

The edifying of the Body of Christ should be primary.

1 Corinthians 14:12 Even so ye, forasmuch as ye are zealous of spiritual *gifts,* seek that ye may excel to the edifying of the church.

Prophecy is important in the life of the Church. Prophecy is the most edifying gift for the Church.

1 Peter 4:10 As every man hath received the gift, *even so* minister the same one to another, as good stewards of the manifold grace of God.

The gift of prophecy is not the same as the office of the prophet. The gift of prophecy is an extension of the Holy Spirit and the Prophet is an extension of the ministry of Christ.

PROPHETIC PREACHING

Preaching with the prophetic gift that is to preach what is directed by the Holy Spirit. If you prepare a sermon and study a subject to preach that is preaching. Many times when I preach I start out preaching I just read my notes and speak. After a while I preach and then I start seeing and hearing in the Spirit and begin to get out of the pages I had prepared. That is now prophetic preaching. Prophetic preaching is not getting the mind of Christ about what to preach. Prophetic preaching includes the preaching of the Word with the prophetic anointing about the people, the atmosphere or even the region. Speaking what God drops in your heart really is what the Church needs in this hour. The preacher does not have to indicate thus saith the Lord as they preach.

1 Peter 4:11 If any man speak, *let him speak* as the oracles of God; if any man minister, *let him do it* as of the ability which God giveth: that God in all things may

be glorified through Jesus Christ, to whom be praise and dominion for ever and ever. Amen.

PROPHETIC SONG

This is an anointing that will rise up within the believer. This gift of prophetic song takes place when a special anointing is in a service. One time in the Litchfield Revival I sung my entire sermon. I tell you it had to be God for this to happen. If this spirit of prophecy is present anyone may prophecy in a meeting. It's the atmosphere of the prophetic anointing. Any saint can operate in a prophetic song.

Colossians 3:16 Let the word of Christ dwell in you richly in all wisdom; teaching and admonishing one another in psalms and hymns and spiritual songs, singing with grace in your hearts to the Lord.

Hebrews 2:12 Saying, I will declare thy name unto my brethren, in the midst of the church will I sing praise unto thee.

God wants to sing to His Church by the Spirit of prophecy. I have prophesied at this level and preached under this anointing. It doesn't always come as a song. Many times it just comes as a rhyme. Everything flows and rhymes like a beautiful song. Prophetic singing is the restoration of the prophetic realm. I don't want just a gift or anointing but the atmosphere of God. The prophetic realm of song comes from where angels sing. Where the Bible talks about "spiritual songs" it is the same as prophetic song.

Ephesians 5:19 Speaking to yourselves in psalms and hymns and spiritual songs, singing and making melody in your heart to the Lord;

PROPHETIC PRESBYTERY

I have to conclude this Chapter with prophetic presbytery. This is the laying on of hands with prophetic ministry of both men and women. It is in short a team of prophetic ministry. These are to be mature Christians whom are anointed by God. When I ordain ministers I love to have multiple prophetic people minister to them. The presbytery does not exclude the individual gifts from God.

This might sound religious but I believe every saint needs a prophetic presbytery for ministry, confirmation and activation.

RELATIONSHIPS

It is easy to allow emotions, desire for love or marriage. There must be unity of spiritual call and ministry compatibility. The number one question should be is it the will of God? Is it the will of God for two to be married? One thing I'd like to put here is out of all the men or women who may go to your Church you only get one for the rest of your life. All the experts of relationships fail to even mention the personal prophecy part of relationships. I believe it has been messed up by those who get to know two people and assume they should be together. I really believe that God has much direction concerning our love or even marriage. It may come in parts but God will speak along these lines. God will speak His will concerning your life including marriage. Each person considering marriage needs a personal Word from the Lord concerning the person they think is it. It might come through personal prophecy, illuminated scripture, dreams and visions. God will speak if you seek Him. Remember that the Holy Spirit will work on both parties. Many times one person will know that God has chosen their mate way before the other.

Many times when we really want that Word concerning our future husband or wife, it will be like no prophetic person will even look at you to minister.

We must remember that God has a process for marriage. It is mutual attraction, friendship, love and a witness of the Holy Spirit. There are always some exceptions to the rule. There are some supernatural prophetic marriages that God just ordained to be together. It happens because God set it up.

GOD'S WAY

Personal prophecy is important in helping Christians make decisions. It is not the only way the Holy Spirit reveals God's will. In the decision making process personal prophecy only plays a part of the role of direction.

The Bible is the ultimate authority and has the final say in all matters. It is the revelation of God in written form as Jesus was the revelation of God in human form. The scriptures contain the thought and intents of God's heart. The Bible was inspired by the Holy Spirit and given to men. The Bible can speak to you and become a rhema now Word. The Bible will line up to what you need to hear. If God speaks to you through scripture it must line up with the biblical standard.

To avoid entering into deception, keep love for the truth and not what you want to selfishly interpret. Our thoughts and desires should not be made into prayers until they receive God's go ahead. If your thoughts or desires don't line up with scripture you will waste your time asking God. These thoughts may be unscriptural, illegal or immoral to divine principles. The Holy Spirit will never tell you what is contrary to scripture. God will not answer false or corrupt prayers.

2 Peter 3:16 As also in all *his* epistles, speaking in them of these things; in which are some things hard to be understood, which they that are unlearned and unstable wrest, as *they do* also the other scriptures, unto their own destruction.

1 John 5:14, 15 And this is the confidence that we have in him, that, if we ask any thing according to his will, he heareth us: And if we know that he hear us, whatsoever we ask, we know that we have the petitions that we desired of him.

If you know your petition is scripturally the will of God, then you will have confidence and faith to believe God for it. Before you accept any thought as from the Lord, make sure it lines up with the Word of God.

No matter what, God's will is to reign supreme in your life. If you serve the Lord, you will do His will.

If you want to succeed in life, ministry and relationships you must be in the will of God. We need guidelines and safeguards for discerning God's will in our lives. If we follow God's orders we will find clarity and direction.

DESIRE

Psalms 40:8 I delight to do thy will, O my God: yea, thy law *is* within my heart.

God desires for you to do His will. He does not enjoy pressuring His children to do His will.

Psalms 37:4 Delight thyself also in the LORD; and he shall give thee the desires of thine heart.

What I've learned the hard way is that God will cause us to change our desires. We will begin to desire what God wants. Prophetic desire is where God plants His will in you and it becomes your will to do His will. A Word is inspired in your spirit, from the Holy Spirit. It is creative ideas inspired by God.

Luke 4:16-21 And he came to Nazareth, where he had been brought up: and, as his custom was, he went into the synagogue on the sabbath day, and stood up for to read. And there was delivered unto him the book of the prophet Esaias. And when he had opened the book, he found the place where it was written, The Spirit of the Lord *is* upon me, because he hath anointed me to preach the gospel to the poor; he hath sent me to heal the brokenhearted, to preach deliverance to the captives, and recovering of sight to the blind, to set at liberty them that are bruised, To preach the acceptable year of the Lord. And he closed the book, and he gave *it* again to the minister, and sat down. And the eyes of all them that were in the synagogue were fastened on him. And he began to say unto them, This day is this scripture fulfilled in your ears.

God uses prophetic people to give specific direction to the Saints. This can come through someone moving in the gift of prophecy or a prophet. If you receive a Word from a true prophet that you know hears from God it can be acted on immediately. We should use care with any word we receive from any source. It is good to meditate on the Word and let God's truth be revealed in your spirit. If the Word comes and it is a witness in your spirit it is most likely something you can act on now. If it does not witness in your spirit, wait for confirmation. The Words I reject are the ones that are unscriptural or clearly not from God.

The Holy Spirit makes known the specific will of God through His gifts to us. The gifts of the Holy Spirit releases information to make wise decisions in business and even parenting. The Holy Spirit causes supernatural provision to come when making right decisions according to the will of God.

To be led by the Holy Spirit is not being led by supernatural manifestations of the gifts.

Isaiah 55:12 For ye shall go out with joy, and be led forth with peace: the mountains and the hills shall break forth before you into singing, and all the trees of the field shall clap *their* hands.

2 Corinthians 5:7 (For we walk by faith, not by sight:)

Romans 8:6 For to be carnally minded *is* death; but to be spiritually minded *is* life and peace.

Colossians 3:15 And let the peace of God rule in your hearts, to the which also ye are called in one body; and be ye thankful.

God is the God of peace and should override all confusion and doubt.

Philippians 4:7 And the peace of God, which passeth all understanding, shall keep your hearts and minds through Christ Jesus.

Psalms 34:14 Depart from evil, and do good; seek peace, and pursue it.

When determining the will of God we should look inside our soul and spirit to see how much peace and joy we have about the situation. The question is do you have more faith or doubt concerning the matter at hand. It is like you will find good fruit within if it is God and bad fruit if it is not God. There is always the rare occasion where there is some demonic interference that can cause a false sense of the fruit within. Most times you will be able to use the peace of God or the lack there of to help you in the direction to go in the things of God. You don't make final decisions until you know inside.

There will be some times like in the life of Paul were we don't know exactly what the Lord wants us to do. We will have to go the way that we believe is best. Paul was going to preach in Asia and God sent him to Macedonia. God has plans of where we go to preach and when we go. To follow God's will we must be sensitive to the Holy Spirit.

Romans 8:16 The Spirit itself beareth witness with our spirit, that we are the children of God:

If you want God's go-ahead then you must have clearance in the spirit. Never ignore the restraints of the Holy Spirit. If you ignore the Holy Spirit it will cause your spiritual senses to become dull. It can also change God's best plans for your life.

God's nature and character is one who reveals His way through His counsel. It is to know God as your Father that watches over His children. Plans go wrong without the counsel of the Lord. Seeking counsel is critical in finding the will of God. God will let His people go ahead without His leading and guiding. It is dangerous to do so because you can step out of God's will and His protection.

Confirmation is the best principle for determining God's will. There is nothing wrong with waiting on the Lord for confirmation. All serious matters should have two or three witnesses before you accept a prophetic Word. It is always necessary that when there is more than one seeking God about something they should be in unity. When everyone is in agreement and peace about a matter it is God's will. We must be in unity with God and among ourselves. We can move forward in confidence based on God's Word, the will of God and confirmation.

God includes His timing, methods and the necessary to do it. The Word gives authorization then God will specify a course of action for you.

Hebrews 6:12 That ye be not slothful, but followers of them who through faith and patience inherit the promises.

Many Words fail because they were not attempted according to God's way.

Isaiah 55:9 For *as* the heavens are higher than the earth, so are my ways higher than your ways, and my thoughts than your thoughts.

God's way can be difficult to determine. The way of God is a time process that must be walked out, because all the details of it rarely are ever revealed ahead of time. Personal prophecies can play a part in revealing the way. The individual pieces of God's puzzle process often fail. Patience is the way of the Lord.

We need special wisdom to do the will of God. Ministry must be released in the fullness of God's timing. If a ministry is not released in the fullness it will fail. There was a time when I invited a prophet to dinner to talk about going into full time ministry. After a long discussion on all the details of ministry, something happened. We were walking out of the restaurant and he s aid to me "if you start your ministry today it will fail." I was so mad at the time but after a little while I knew he was right. I was not committed to a local Church, had things in my heart yet to deal with, there wasn't the peace of God and I was not in God's perfect way. I thank God for that sure Word prophet. It was one year later that I started my ministry and all of the ways of God were lined up.

Our action must be according to God's unusual plan. Many times God's way is not practical. Some people receive great prophecies but never find God's way to do it. At the same time some find their way and act according to God's plan. You can know God's perfect way but if you begin to revert to old ways, you will step out of the anointing to bring it to pass. Once a Word has given approval, we must wait for the way to come or we will not see the fulfillment.

Psalms 27:11 Teach me thy way, O LORD, and lead me in a plain path, because of mine enemies.

God has a time for every work and the way to accomplish it.

CAREFUL DECISIONS

We will receive many prophetic Words and we will need to be careful of the decisions we make. We need to be careful before taking action to buy, sell, move or making critical decisions. We should never take final action until God has confirmed. We need to be led by the Holy Spirit and inspired, motivated by personal prophecy. Being led of the spirit and participating in personal prophecy does not mean that we become all about everything is a sign from God. If we get to the place that everything we see and hear in the natural is God speaking to u s it can get us off track. I have known very prophetic people that begin to see every letter on a billboard, truck or whatever as God's way of speaking. God can speak in many ways. Biblically God speaks through hearing, sensing, seeing and knowing in the spirit. If we replace the way we hear from God with the natural, its source can make the word corrupt. This is what I call spooky Christians. When God speaks to you about major decisions, you want confirmation but if you look at every billboard, car lettering etc. to confirm you cannot know it's from God. Use the bible as your guide and many of God's prophetic ways to confirm to you prophecies from God. If you need confirmation let it come from scripture, preaching of the Word, inner peace, prophetic Word etc.

UNDERSTANDING PROPHETIC

We should all want to make decisions in the will of God. God wants to speak prophetically but do not allow personal prophecy to become a substitute for seeking God. Personal prophecy is not to take place of the inner voice of the Holy Spirit. The gifts of the Holy Spirit are an extension of God communicating the mind of Christ to individuals within the Body of Christ.

Prophecy is not for play. God will not answer questions that can be resolved by diligently seeking scripture. God doesn't respond to foolish questions. We want the prophetic people to answer the question like, whom will I marry, when will I get my home or is my family member in Heaven or hell? If the answer to these question were not what the people would want to hear, why would the prophetic person answer them.

God usually speaks prophetically only those things about the future which we need to know in order to make proper decisions. It is scriptural for a person to go to a prophet, having faith that God will supernaturally meet their need. You can ask questions and expect answers.

But your motives, your attitude and your question must be proper to receive results. You should seek God first and look in scripture and that will prepare you to receive.

If you have come to a prophetic meeting to hear about something specific don't be disappointed if you don't hear new revelation. If you seek God first, it will cause the prophetic Word to bring you confirmation. This will give you greate r confidence in your ability to hear from God yourself, it will cause you to receive the Word by faith and that will activate the power of the fulfillment of that Word.

It is necessary that you have some idea of how a prophetic person may give you confirmation. It may be yes or no or maybe even that you need to wait for the answer is on the way.

KEEP RECORD

If you handle your prophetic Words correctly in attitude and action you will have the full benefits of prophecy.

Over the years I have received many prophecies and they were not all recorded. Once I realized the importance of recording God's Word, I have worked to record every prophecy. In the first years of ministry we went through thousands of cassette tapes. We should thank God that recording equipment is available. It doesn't matter how awesome the personal prophecy is, we can never process it and really understand what God is saying. This is why this Chapter is so important.

How much value do you put in what God speaks to you? We can only remember some of the prophecy. Recording the sound of the personal prophecy is the number one thing we all need to do. If someone says they have a Word for you it should be recorded. If there is no equipment to record available then have them write it out. A true prophetic minister will honor that request if it's from God. If we are in a meeting and the prophetic person isn't being recorded then write it out yourself as much detail as you can remember.

Many times if you have many personal prophecies, they will have similar thoughts of God in parts of the Words. This will help us confirm they are from God. When God says something again and again in different ways He wants us to get it. This is both in personal prophecy and the written Word.

I record all the Words I give for the person receiving and my benefit. Some Words I've released have been twisted by the person receiving. It is safe to record for me because if someone says I said something, I have a recording that will confirm or redeem me from allegation. It is personal protection to record prophecies.

We should record each prophecy and write them out. The bible says to write the vision down so that it is plain to see. We should not make major decisions based on a prophecy until we know it is what God meant.

After we record the prophecy that is when we judge and evaluate the prophecy. I don't judge quickly because some Words seem false but after study of the Word it was from God.

Romans 8:16 The Spirit itself beareth witness with our spirit, that we are the children of God:

You only witness prophecy with your spirit. We do not discern prophecy with our mind, opinions, will, emotions, desires or goals. Our beliefs are not true witness to prophecy. Our spirit bears witness. You don't even have to understand personal prophecy. We lean not on our own understanding.

If prophecy is from God it will come to pass and we fulfill God's will.

It has been the belief that God only speaks what will confirm that which has already been put in our spirit. When Samuel told David he would be king, David was going about with no idea according to scripture of this in his spirit. This is just one and this belief will block a lot of fresh new revelation from personal prophecy. We can't reject prophecy simply because we never even thought of what was being prophesied. If we receive new thoughts in personal prophecy write them out and pray. We shoul d remain open because God's Words are progressive and we may miss that next level if we close ourselves to new things.

I prophesied to a couple that their child was being healed of an immune problem and it was going to be a miracle. The parents knew nothing was wrong with their child. They hang on to the Word and months later the child got pneumonia and they got the Word out and the miracle came to pass. We cannot limit God.

We can take our personal prophecy as a Word from the Lord and war a good warfare with it that will cause the perfect will of God. If we believe God we will be established and if we believe God's prophets we will prosper.

The thing we are to do with personal prophecy is to keep doing what we have been doing unless God has stated to do otherwise. It doesn't matter how many great things that you have been told.

When prophecy is released with instructions there is an anointing for action. I received a prophecy in my first year as a Christian that said I would have miracles, signs and wonders following me. The thing that I didn't hear until years later was the action part of the Word. I played the tape and the prophecy stated that I was to study to show myself approved and then miracles, signs and wonders would follow me. There was an action that had to happen to get me to that place.

After we receive prophecy we need to meditate on it, witness to it, war for it and act if directed to do so

REMOVING HINDRANCES

Prophecy is conditional and we have to cooperate with God to bring the Word to pass. The biggest thing that you must understand is that there are many hindrances to prophecy. There are many spiritual and personal hindrances that are meant to block you from the fulfillment of prophecies.

The first one I want to talk about is inpatients. We always want it now. Personal prophecy is not going to come to pass in our time but God's. Do you want to be in a desert like Moses for forty years? Every time we fail to wait patiently until God reveals His divine way. We have to wait until God's appointed time for prophecy is fulfilled.

God knows all the things that must happen before our prophecies can come to pass. We are to take it one step at a time.

I also have seen many people that always have someone to blame for a problem. If we get mad and blame someone for a problem it can cause us to get mad at God and everyone else. This in turn can cause the final result in not receiving the promise of the Lord.

Many Christians seem to keep a mindset that will hinder prophecy. Preconceived ideas will not allow personal prophecies to change our way of thinking. People reject a prophecy just because of a mindset.

Look at this,
Matthew 18:21-22 Then came Peter to him, and said, Lord, how oft shall my brother sin against me, and I forgive him? till seven times? Jesus saith unto him, I say not unto thee, Until seven times: but, Until seventy times seven.

Even when Jesus talked to the disciples about the death and resurrection they rejected it. It didn't line up with their thinking.

In the Litchfield Revival God spoke that it would end and they didn't receive it. It went against their mindset.

If it was up to Jesus' disciples He would have never went to the cross. How many of us are stuck in a mindset about something in our lives.

I have seen the most powerful self hindrance is pride. It is the most dangerous of fulfillment of personal prophecy. Pride if we let it will do more than just hinder personal prophecy but it can destroy our ministry from ever coming into its fullness.

Unbelief is always there trying to convince us that what we may know to be true is false. Unbelief means that you once believed and now don't believe. If you ever feel like you have been in a desert place for a long time you may be dealing with unbelief.

I know for me I have dealt with procrastination when it comes to fulfilling personal prophecies. Putting off what God has told us to do can get us in trouble. We need to act on what we can do so God will do what we cannot do.

If we deal with a poor self image it can altar our personal prophecies. If we have a complex we can really mishandle the Words from God. God will have a harder time convincing someone of something that has a poor self image.

When people are trying for years to make something happen, but nothing happens. The soul will try to defend itself by rejecting prophecy. We don't want to be disappointed again and we reject the prophecy. If you get a defeated spirit it hinders prophecy. Remember we need to guard our heart, mind and emotions. God is faithful to watch over His Word to perform it.

When you receive a personal prophecy it most likely will seem impossible. We need to focus on the promise rather than the evidence and we will step into God's opportunity. God loves to see us through the impossibilities.

If we want personal prophecy to come to pass we must respond properly. I want to deal with the hindrance of improper response. We limit the power and prophetic promise by an improper response to the Word. If a prophetic person tells us something that we are to do, we should do it. Obedience is the only way to fulfill God's promise.

Matthew 13:3-13 And he spake many things unto them in parables, saying, Behold, a sower went forth to sow; And when he sowed, some *seeds* fell by the way side, and the fowls came and devoured them up: Some fell upon stony places, where they had not much earth: and forthwith they sprung up, because they had no deepness of earth: And when the sun was up, they were scorched; and because they had no root, they withered away. And some fell among thorns; and the thorns sprung up, and choked them: But other fell into good ground, and brought forth fruit, some an hundredfold, some sixtyfold, some thirtyfold. Who hath ears to hear, let him hear. And the disciples came, and said unto him, Why speakest thou unto them in parables? He answered and said unto them, Because it is given unto you to know the mysteries of the kingdom of heaven, but to them it is not given. For whosoever hath, to him shall be given, and he shall have more abundance: but whosoever hath not, from him shall be taken away even that he hath. Therefore speak I to them in parables: because they seeing see not; and hearing they hear not, neither do they understand.

We can have such improper responses to the Word by the ability to retain the Word that can cause us to a weak response. This is the heart of the selfish people pleaser. Another improper response is worldly (a life of sin) and it causes personal prophecies to be chocked out and kills God's plans for a person. You can receive prophecy and be in the world (living in sin) but it doesn't mean God will force His will on anyone.

Another hindrance is misinterpretation and manipulation of prophecy. We can hear from God and how we apply the Word can hinder it from coming to pass. We can take prophecy to lightly by not following it seriously. Personal prophecy is nothing to play with. You can not manipulate the Word. I've seen people try to personally cause prophecies to come to pass. God accepts no substitute for obedience, regardless of how beneficial it may seem.

Sometimes the blockage is in the soul of a man. This consists of emotion, desire or ambition. We can let our emotions hinder God's Words from the fulfillment and fear man instead of God.

Jeremiah 38:19 And Zedekiah the king said unto Jeremiah, I am afraid of the Jews that are fallen to the Chaldeans, lest they deliver me into their hand, and they mock me.

1 Samuel 15:24 And Saul said unto Samuel, I have sinned: for I have transgressed the commandment of the LORD, and thy words: because I feared the people, and obeyed their voice.

Our feelings can prevent us from faith for the Word when we have a personal dislike for the person giving the Word or the prophecy.

When things don't work out the way we want disappointment can hinder fulfillment of God's Word. If you have had disappointments it can cause you to expect to be disappointed. It can cause a lack of faith for the Word. We must be willing to wait despite apparent failure of the prophecy and willing to go through God's process.

There are many spiritual hindrances where prophecies are concerned. You can read about them all in the "Defeating the Demonic Realm"

FINA L WORD

God desires to speak to His children. God speaks to us in many ways. We must remember that prophecies are conditional. We are to covet prophecy which is holding it near and dear to your heart. When God speaks His plans He will do it His way. Personal prophecy is just part of God's plan. When we are at the right place, doing the right thing, hearing and speaking the right Words the spirit will bear witness to God's will.

In this day God is raising up accompany of believers who know their God and shall do great exploits. This is the perfect timing for the Five-Fold Ministry to be fully restored to the Church. The Saints of God need to be matured and ready for battle in this day. Christian's maturity and sensitivity are no longer an option. If Christians want to be overcomers they need to get ready.

Sooner or later we can't blame everything on demons. We have to take responsibility for our own actions & why do I keep going down this road? How are they getting in and driving me? What are my open doors?

Cheating, Stealing, Abuse of Spouses (whether is physical or through words) Lust, Lying, Letting others control you, Religion or defending the religious ALL OPEN DOORS

Ask yourself why are you in the place that you are? Am I really letting God have full reign in my life? Am I letting Him mold me and make me in his image?

GOD OPPOSSES THE PROUD, BUT GIVES GRACE TO THE HUMBLE

If you are really letting God change you then there should be fruit. Are you BAD FRUIT or GOOD FRUIT? If you are still in the same place with sin & bondage & not dealing with things as god wants you to then that's BAD FRUIT

If you are out of the pit, encouraging to others, overcoming sin & bondage, overcoming demonic forces, if you are a testimony to others then you are producing GOOD FRUIT

If you speak prophetically GOD always follows up with encouragement.

If you don't deal with the issue's that you have and want to run instead let me remind you that all roads will end up to the same place and that would be the path that GOD wants for you. So running will only prolong the inevitable. You can run but you can't hide from God.

We are at a place that if you don't want to deal with the issues & don't want DELIVERANCE, then you can't expect God to fulfill His promises. We can't have any hindrances for the new level of GLORY that is coming.

Walking through every door is not GOD sometimes doors will open to trip you up and it becomes a distraction from the REAL PURPOSE.

Sooner or later you will have to deal with the issues. You can't be or do anything for God with a bunch of junk in the way.

Revival Waves of Glory Ministries is going somewhere to a level we haven't been before & demons & GLORY can't go together. This should be the same for all of God's children.

ABOUT THE AUTHOR

Bill Vincent was born 12/25/73 in Illinois. Bill had a lot of challenges as a child. Bill was the teenager parents didn't want their children to hang with. Bill was invited to a prophetic service about 1990 and after he went that was the service that changed his life. Bill was born again and ministered to for the first time. The man that prophesied to Bill that day was Dennis Goodell of International Miracle Ministries. Dennis Goodell has now gone on to be with the Lord.

Bill was a servant to Dennis Goodell for about ten years and had seen and experienced a great deal of miracles. This was the man Bill received an impartation of gifts of the Holy Spirit.

Bill was trained within the Church for many years. Bill's prophetic gift was matured and sharpened. Bill was ordained in 2001 while being a minister within the Church. Bill continued ministering in the Church and other places. In 2001 Bill established a Church in Litchfield, IL.

This ministry traveled as the Lord led. Bill operated in the prophetic with words of knowledge for healing spirit, soul and body. In 2008 Bill was frustrated and sought God for something fresh. After a couple of months God showed up with His mighty presence. August 2008 a Revival started. God's presence got stronger and stronger. After a few months God began to show up with mighty miracles, healing, signs and wonders. The revival continued for over two years. There were many miracles and signs every week. There were testimonies of Cancers healed, tumors removed, arthritis healed and many other creative miracles.

Bill has an accurate prophetic gift, a powerful revelatory preaching anointing with miracles signs and wonders following.

Bill started a ministry by the name of Revival Waves of Glory Ministries in 2010. This ministry is a ministry with a fresh vision. God has brought Bill through much adversity. This ministry has already had signs and wonders with deep prophetic ministry. Bill is a Prophet of God with a true Apostolic Anointing. Bill has authored many books, established a School of ministry called The School of the Supernatural and created a book publishing company called Revival Waves of Glory Books & Publishing.

Bill has found the glory of God in an awesome way. He has a special relationship with the father and powerful revelatory, healing and prophetic anointings.

RECOMMENDED BOOKS

By Bill Vincent
Overcoming Obstacles
Uncovering God's Glory
Defeating the Demonic Realm
Increasing Your Prophetic Gift
A Greater Anointing
Receiving Your Miracle
The Supernatural Realm
Waves of Revival
Revelatory Restoration
Resurrection Power
Called of God
Discovering Breakthrough
Increasing God's Glory
Love is Waiting—Don't Let Love Pass You By
Signs & Wonders
Healing Training Manual
Rapture Revelations
Expanding God's Glory

By Bill Vincent, Paula Loveless, Joseph Basurto, Dawn Vitale and Jackie Money
Experience God's Love

By Bishop Gregory Leachman
God's Greatest Challenge:
Man & His Ungodly Ways

By Richard Money
My Life in a Salami Factory

www.ingramcontent.com/pod-product-compliance
Lightning Source LLC
Chambersburg PA
CBHW052106070526
44584CB00017B/2365